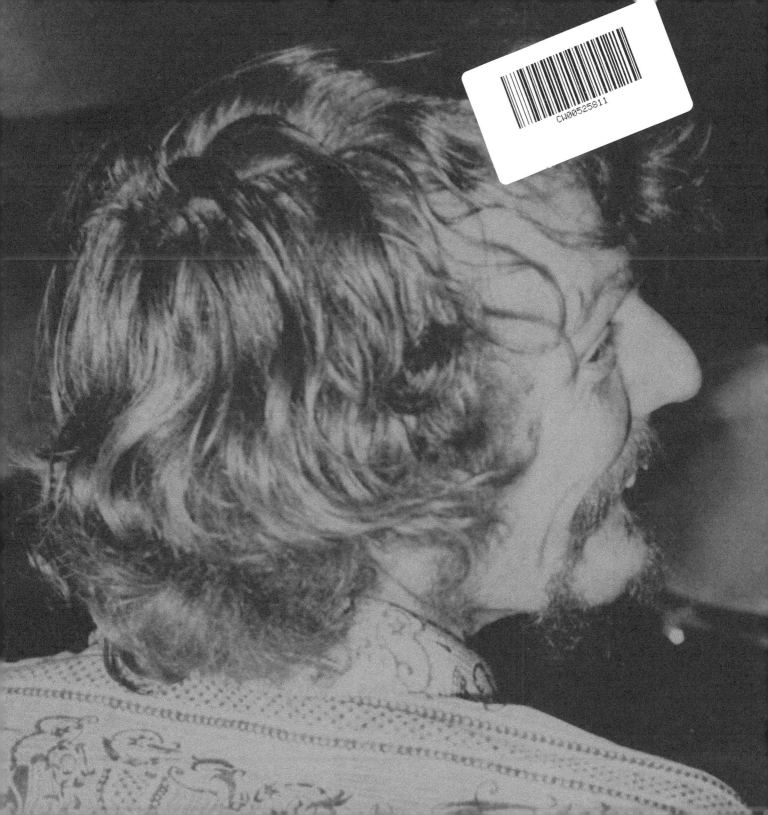

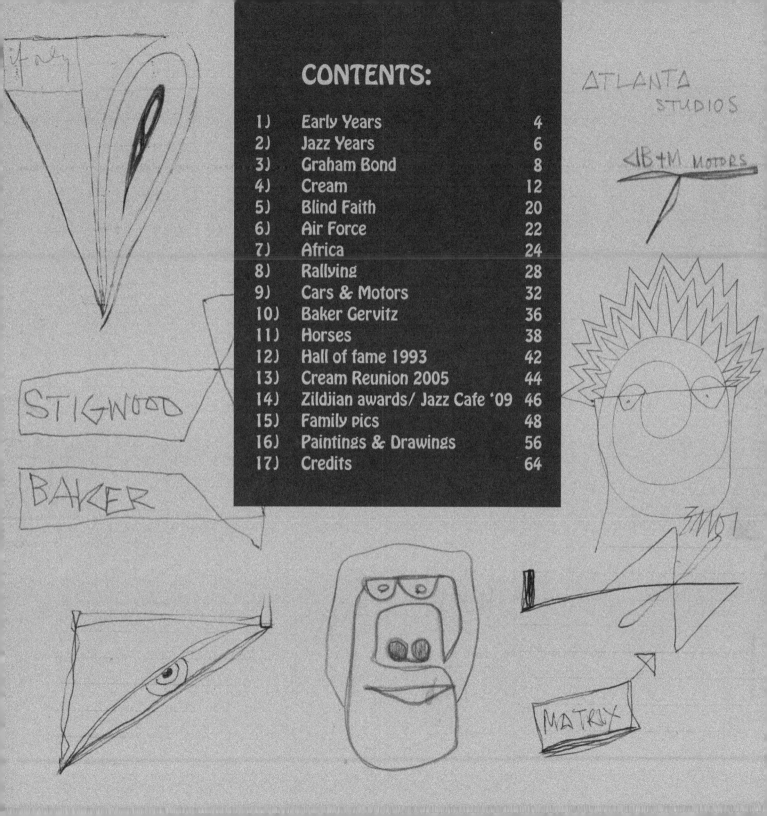

CONTENTS:

With my Dad Ted Baker...

Stockholm, Norrbro and Vaktparaden
The North Bridge and the Royal Guard

Dear Mr and Mrs Finch,
As you can see we're now in Stockholm. This is a wonderful city: it has to be seen to be believed. Beautiful building built on unhewn rocks and fly over roads and everything. The big trouble here is that it's so cold 6°below freezing. Still, further north, it is 58°F below freezing!! I'm glad I'm not there. We had and 11½ hours train journey here yesterday in the same train all the time as well! That was a bit of a drag as you can imagine. This hotel is even more luxurious than the others with radios in the rooms and dials on the wall which you set to whatever to you want to be awakened. Also marvellous showers. You'd like the food here even more than Denmark. They certainly knows how to eat out here! Hows fatty cat I keeping himself: still fat and lazy and keeping himself nice and warm. He wouldn't like it here abit. The pavement is covered with about 4 inches of ice. It's very slippery. There isn't much snow here just lots of ice. See you. Love Ginger.

MR & MRS E. FINCH

10 ELM WAY, NEASDEN

LONDON, N.W.10

ENGLAND.

STOCKHOLM 8
28. 3. 56
BREV B

Early Years...

Dad's grave...

238513 L. CPL.
F. L. F. BAKER
ROYAL SIGNALS
15TH NOVEMBER 1943 AGE 28

Dear Mr & Mrs Finch,

We finished the tour yesterday afternoon as OSLO and ODENSE were both cancelled for reasons unknown to us. Sweden is a wonderful country with big lakes, mountains and huge forests. Göteborg is about W.S.W. of Stockholm on the opposite coast so we travelled right across Sweden. All the lakes were frozen and there was a lot of snow in the countryside. The little houses in the villages we really great. It's a wonderful place. The hotel at GÖTEBORG was in the middle of a big park and was very good. They called us over our room radios to wake us in the morning. We were very sorry to part with Sister as she is a truly great woman. Still all good things come to an end. Give my regards to Simon with love Ginger.

MR & MRS. E. FINCH,

10 ELM WAY, NEASDEN,

LONDON, N.W.10.,

ENGLAND.

Jazz Years...
1958-Graham Bond Organization

77/78/1
SIDE ONE

MILENBERG JOYS
(Rapollo, Mares, Merton)
The Storyville Jazzmen

Bob Wallis, tpt; John
Mortimer, tbn; Les
Wood, clt; Hugh
Rainey, bjo; Stu Winsey,
bass; Ginger Baker,
dms; Pete Gresham,
piano

Supervision:
Brian R. Harvey

77 RECORDS
78 R.P.M.

My first recording with
The Storyville Jazzmen....

6

Graham Bond Organization

"Within weeks, we were in the Decca Studio's at West Hampstead and the album 'The Sound of '65' was recorded in less than a week. I did the artwork one night after the sessions." (Hellraiser)

COLUMBIA

COLUMBIA GRAPHOPHONE CO LTD ALL RIGHTS OF THE MANUFACTURER AND OF THE OWNER OF THE RECORDED WORK

SOUTHERN
MUSIC
NCB
7XCA 27568

℗ 1965

SOLD IN U.K. SUBJECT TO
RESALE PRICE CONDITIONS
SEE PRICE LISTS

TELL ME (I'M GONNA LOVE AGAIN)
(John Group)
THE GRAHAM BOND
ORGANISATION

MADE IN GT. BRITAIN

7XCA 27568

BOND

GRAHAM

BLUES

The Sound of '65

The Graham Bond Organization

33SX
1711

A Robert Stigwood
Production

SIDE ONE

1 HOOCHIE COOCHIE *(Dixon)*
2 BABY MAKE LOVE TO ME *(Group-Godfrey)*
3 NEIGHBOUR NEIGHBOUR
4 EARLY IN THE MORNING *(Trad.-arr. Group)*
5 SPANISH BLUES *(Group)*
6 OH BABY *(Group)*
7 LITTLE GIRL *(Group)*

SIDE TWO

1 I WANT YOU *(Group)*
2 WADE IN THE WATER *(Trad.-arr. Group)*
3 GOT MY MOJO WORKING *(Morganfield)*
4 TRAIN TIME *(Group)*
5 BABY BE GOOD TO ME *(Group-Godfrey)*
6 HALF A MAN *(Group)*
7 TAMMY *(Evans-Livingston)*

Cover Design : Ginger Baker
Sleevenote : Chris Welch

© 1965

This record marks the break-through of the unique and exciting music of the Graham Bond Organization. It will bring wider appreciation for their startling fusion of rhythm and blues and modern jazz, which until now, only club and concert audiences have experienced

The extraordinary variety of sounds, styles and treatments that Graham's band can attain are brilliantly showcased in this, their first album, which will surprise new listeners and delight their devoted fans.

The Organization formed early in 1963 when all four left Alexis Korner's Blues Incorporated. It was natural that the new group should give a jazz feel to their music. Graham has already been voted second in the 1961 Melody Maker readers' poll, 'New Star' section, and had made his name playing alto saxophone with the Don Rendell Quintet.

The other members of the group, Ginger Baker, Jack Bruce and Dick Heckstall-Smith have all played in various jazz groups. But as renegade jazzmen they turned to rhythm and blues with such fervency and played with such a combination of skill and emotion, they quickly built up a massive following in live appearances up and down the country.

One of those rare groups in which each member is indispensable, they all make a vital contribution to the overall sound.

Graham leads on organ and vocals and occasionally returns to alto sax, which he plays simultaneously with the organ, and what an impressive sight he makes !

Good-looking Jack Bruce lays the solid foundation of bass guitar beat and is being featured more and more on harmonica and as a singer.

Peak-capped Dick Heckstall-Smith, riffs and wails on tenor saxophone, and the explosive Ginger Baker propels the group with his dynamic and completely personal drum technique.

They are musicians who are technically brilliant and at the same time emotionally responsive, to such a degree that they can produce sounds that a few years ago would not have been believed possible by British musicians. It is unlikely there is another group like them in the world.

Sophisticated, raw, savage and soulful, their music is all these things. It is the music of the Graham Bond Organization—The Sound of '65.

LONG PLAY 33⅓ R.P.M • **E.M.I. RECORDS LIMITED**
(Controlled by Electric & Musical Industries Ltd.)
HAYES · MIDDLESEX · ENGLAND
Made and Printed in Great Britain

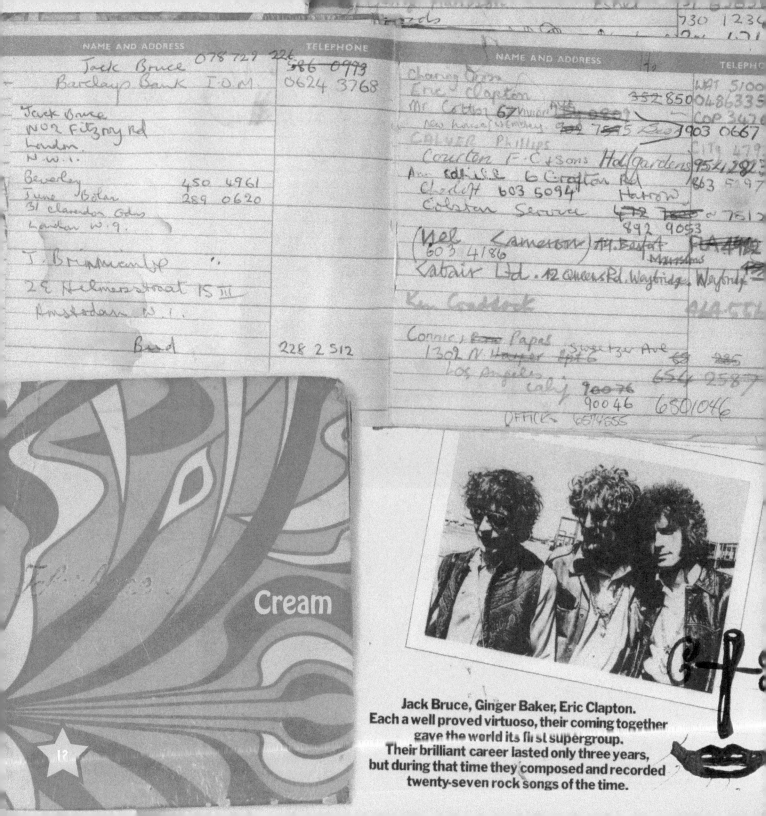

Jack Bruce   078 727 226
Barclays Bank I.O.M.   586 0993
    0624 3768

Jack Bruce
No2 Fitzroy Rd
London
N.W.1.

Beverley   450 4961
June Bolan   289 0620
31 Clarendon Gdns
London W.9.

J. Brinnacintop   "
2E Helmersstraat 15 III
Amsterdam N.1.

    Bird   228 2512

Charing Cross   WAT 5100
Eric Clapton   352 8500 486335
Mr Cotton 67 .... Ave   COP 3476
new house Wembley   903 0667
GALVER Phillips   CITY 479
Courton F.C & Sons Hol Gardens   954 2823
Ann ...... 6 Crofton Rd   863 5997
Cardiff   603 5094   Harrow
Colston Service   7812
    892 9053
(Mel Cameron) M. Beyfort   ....
603 4186   Mansions
Katair Ltd. 12 Queens Rd. Weybridge. Weybridge
Ken Craddock   414556
Connie, Papas   Swetzer Ave
1302 N. Harper Apt 6   685
Los Angeles   654 2587
    Calif 90076
    90046   6801046
OFFICE 667455

730 1234

Cream

Jack Bruce, Ginger Baker, Eric Clapton.
Each a well proved virtuoso, their coming together
gave the world its first supergroup.
Their brilliant career lasted only three years,
but during that time they composed and recorded
twenty-seven rock songs of the time.

12

"Eric & I became close friends. We went on a shopping spree in Portobello Road & found a clothing Emporium called Lord Kitchener's Valet where we purchased military coats decorated with frogging."
(Hellraiser)

laxed. Don't gradually
Keep time!

Care should be taken when used. A good rule of thumb is mammy daddy on the single stroke on tom-toms.

Ginger Baker's Drum Book

I enjoyed painting these drumskins...(GB)

...ade a complete mess of it. I could only play it fast
...ften easier to play things fast as the speed disguise
...ork and concentration I got it together and found
... Diddles" even faster and as near to perfection as
...drummer has to be able to play everything at any

...ments. These you find in any drum tutor – not quit

...ally comfortable leading with the left hand as the
...th both hands – you can never have the problem o
...good hand – enabling total freedom to play wha

...ur right stick is striking your left stick is high. This
...tion.
...e with your foot (feet) when practising.
...tirely up to how one feels most comfortable.
...ay the basic rudiments might be tempted to jus
...er, just a quick glance through as there are a few
...the basics.
...e before part two.
...there are 26 basic rudiments. In this book there
...d I feel that the extra 5 are basic rudiments.

This is one instance where spee

R L R L R L R L   R L R L R L
L R L R L R L R   L R L R L R

Keep all beats even and hands rel

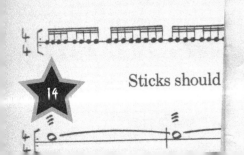

Sticks should

TUNING THE DRUMS

This is very much up to the individual, I tune my drums to be in tune with th
band as much as possible. Obviously you can't be in tune with a band when a lot o
different keys are used. However, if you tune your drums to fit most keys used, this is th
best you can do.

I tune the tom toms a fifth apart, the large tom tom on the tonic, the small one
fifth up. You'll find that as you play them they go flat and usually only one or tw
tighteners need taking up – usually those nearest to you as this is where you're likely to hi
the rim. When using two small and two large tom toms I tune through the octave, th
lowest and highest one octave apart, the other large drum one third up, and the othe
small drum on the fifth. I don't use dampers (on tom toms) as I like the drums to ring. I als
block the breather hole with a nut and bolt. It's a good thing to get the bass player to hel
you tune up. The snare drum and bass drums are not so important to actually be in tun
here, the important thing is the sound. Bass drums nearly always need damping
otherwise they boom too much. When using two bass drums I like to have them on tw
different sounds. The snare drum should sound crisp and clear.

CLEANING CYMBALS

In order to get the best sound from your cymbals it really does help if they are cleane
regularly. Great care should be taken with this as to use metal polish or detergent ca
adversely affect the true sound. First one should wash the cymbals using a soft nail br

Toad.

Peter Baker

Guitar chords used in this composition

E   D   A

Drums

GINGER BAKER

reference reco
STUDIO Liberty SPEED: 45   TIMING:
MONO

FALSTAFF BEER
The Cream

(JAMING)

BILLY PRESTON
+ CO.

"...in March 1969, I did some tracks
in the studio with Billy Preston and
George Harrison. We were doing
'That's the Way God Planned it' when
our roadie Mick Turner popped his
head round the door to tell me that
my son had just been born in The
Avenue Road Clinic in St John's Wood'.
(Hellraiser)

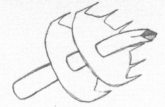

PRESSED RAT & WARTHOG

BLUE CONDITION

MAD JACK

E.R.A. 17171.

ITS RAINING AND SO IS SHE.

DOWN... DOWN THRO'... DOWN UPON ENTERING FASTEN SEAT BELTS: THE
LINING OF FOR STUMAC -- PREPARE FOR STORM TIME TAKE DOWN! S.T.T.D.

ROUGH FOAM-FLECKED OILY-DARK PURPLE-PRE-STORM SEA — BREAKS —
SCATTERING ITS VERY PIEZES OVER A VERY LARGE AREA... 8 HRS NON-STOP
SOMETIMES — STROBOSCOPIK LITENING FLICKERS ILLUMINATING BLACK-BLUE-
SILVER SUDDEN SHAPES — INCONSISTENT THUNDER: LITENING CRACKS-CLAPS
JOINED BY A HOWLING — NOW STILL—WIND.

ITS STILL RAINING AND SO IS SHE.

⬛⬛⬛⬛ DOWN TAKE TIME STORM PREPARE AND STUMAC FOR LINING!

APREZ STORM TIME MUDDY-BROWN-GREY SEA — FULL-O-COCONUTS
AND OTHER DEBRIS — SWIRLS DOWN ROUND THRO' ROCKS — THINKING —
WHO BROKE MY CLOUD? THE ANGEL HARPY!
WHO BROKEN OUT-O-DOWN-THRO'-INTO-OUT-O-ME?
WAIT TIL IT CLEARS AND DEAR OLE SOL LOOKS DOWN AND SMILES ON DOWN
AND DOWN THRO'
HAVE A DOLLY-MIXTURE — IT WON'T HELP BUT IT SURE TASTES GOOD.
ITS STILL RAINING — SO IS SHE.
INTO THRO' DOWN ON:—ARMS — BACK — LEGS ACHE AND SHIVER —— EARS, EYES,
EMPTY HEADLESS HEAD ACHE — EVERY BLOODY BONE ACHE. EYES, NOSE, BOWELS STREAM
AND STILL IT RAINS ·AND SO DOES SHE.
ATISHOO — ATASHAAAH —— ACHOOOPPP —— AHACHAAA! HOW MUCH LONGER?
WAIT AND SEE — WAIT 'TIL IT CLEARS AND DEAR OLE SOL SHINES SMILING—

DOWN AND DOWN THRU!
THE WIND AGAIN
ARE WE THERE
FEELS NEAR.
HOW LONG HAS IT BIN!
18 HRS SINCE S.T.T.D. NEARLY 5 DAYS
SINCE CUFO-K. (COUNT-UP-FALL-OFF—KAALVORAK)
MY HEADS FALLING OFF! I COULD DO WIF SUM O THAT LOCAL HOME GROWN MADNESS

I've always had a passion for the written word. Sci-fi pros, Lyrics and letters...

16

BLUE CONDITION

DON'T TAKE THE WRONG DIRECTION PASSING THROUGH
INSTEAD OF DEEP REFLECTION OF WHAT'S TRUE
FOR IT'S A COMBINATION OF JUDGMENTS MADE BY YOU

NO RELAXATION, NO CONVERSATION, NO VARIATION
IN A VERY DARK BLUE, BLUE CONDITION.

EARLY RISING EVERY DAY
YOU MUST BE ENTERPRISING IN YOUR WAY
OR YOU WILL HEAR NO LAUGHTER OR SEE THE SUN
LIFE WILL BE ONE DISASTER ALL THE WAY THROUGH

NO RELAXATION, NO CONVERSATION, NO VARIATION,
IN A VERY DARK BLUE, BLUE CONDITION.

PRESSED RAT AND WARTHOG

PRESSED RAT AND WARTHOG HAVE CLOSED DOWN THEIR SHOP
THEY DIDN'T WANT TO, 'TWAS ALL THEY HAD GOT.
SELLING ATONAL APPLES, AMPLIFIED HEAT
AND PRESSED RATS COLLECTION OF DOG LEGS AND FEET.

SADLY THEY LEFT TELLING NO ONE GOODBYE
PRESSED RAT WORE RED JODHPURS WARTHOG A STRIPED TIE
BETWEEN THEM THEY CARRIED A THREE LEGGED SACK
WENT STRAIGHT ON ROUND A CORNER AND NEVER CAME BACK.

PRESSED RAT AND WARTHOG HAVE CLOSED DOWN THEIR SHOP
THE BAD CAPTAIN MADMAN HAD TOLD THEM TO STOP
SELLING ATONAL APPLES, AMPLIFIED HEAT,
AND PRESSED RATS COLLECTION OF DOG LEGS AND FEET.

THE BAD CAPTAIN MADMAN HAD ORDERED THEIR FATE
HE LAUGHED AND STOMPED OFF WITH A NAUGHTICAL GATE
THE GATE TURNED INTO A DEROGA TREE
AND HIS PEGLEG GOT WOODWORM AND BROKE INTO THREE.

PRESSED RAT AND WARTHOG HAVE CLOSED DOWN THEIR SHOP
THEY DIDN'T WANT TO, 'TWAS ALL THEY HAD GOT
SELLING ATONAL APPLES, AMPLIFIED HEAT,
AND PRESSED RATS COLLECTION OF DOG LEGS AND FEET.

HOTELL Malmen
STOCKHOLM/SWEDEN

the time this reaches you there'll only be three weeks left for me to do.

Last night I left my towel, soap, shaving soap, razor, after shave lotion, toothbrush and tooth paste at the K.B. Hall. Isn't the typical of your ginger haired monster? Now I've got to buy all that gear again. How bad!

This is a laughing dancing elephant. Bass playing Tone is like this when he's a wee bitty high. We call him jumbo. He got a photo and and a paragraph in a Copenhagen paper this morning for his antics on the stage at the K.B. Hall last night. He's one of the greatest showmen I've seen. He keeps us all in fits. When he's high he's even better.

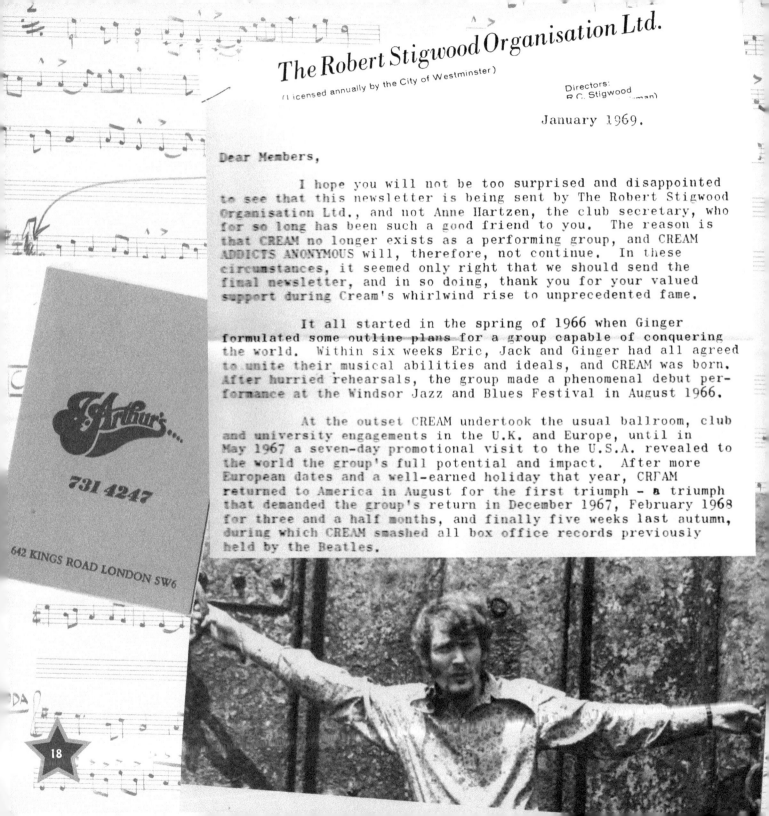

The Robert Stigwood Organisation Ltd.

(Licensed annually by the City of Westminster)

Directors:
R.C. Stigwood
(~~~man)

January 1969.

Dear Members,

I hope you will not be too surprised and disappointed to see that this newsletter is being sent by The Robert Stigwood Organisation Ltd., and not Anne Hartzen, the club secretary, who for so long has been such a good friend to you. The reason is that CREAM no longer exists as a performing group, and CREAM ADDICTS ANONYMOUS will, therefore, not continue. In these circumstances, it seemed only right that we should send the final newsletter, and in so doing, thank you for your valued support during Cream's whirlwind rise to unprecedented fame.

It all started in the spring of 1966 when Ginger formulated some outline plans for a group capable of conquering the world. Within six weeks Eric, Jack and Ginger had all agreed to unite their musical abilities and ideals, and CREAM was born. After hurried rehearsals, the group made a phenomenal debut performance at the Windsor Jazz and Blues Festival in August 1966.

At the outset CREAM undertook the usual ballroom, club and university engagements in the U.K. and Europe, until in May 1967 a seven-day promotional visit to the U.S.A. revealed to the world the group's full potential and impact. After more European dates and a well-earned holiday that year, CREAM returned to America in August for the first triumph - a triumph that demanded the group's return in December 1967, February 1968 for three and a half months, and finally five weeks last autumn, during which CREAM smashed all box office records previously held by the Beatles.

J. Arthur's....

731 4247

642 KINGS ROAD LONDON SW6

Here I am writing music at the oak dining table in Harrow, circa 1969/70. In mid 1970, not long before he died, "I invited Jimi [Hendrix] over to my house for dinner. Jimi arrived on time with [a] beautiful blonde. Liz had cooked a sumptuous meal and we sat around our antique farmhouse table"
(GB & Hellraiser)

WINWOOD
Out of Traffic , the coast is clear.

GRECH
The family man.

BAKER
Blind Faith lean thumper.

CLAPTON
Central nervous system.

Blind Faith

"The Blind Faith album was brilliant, one of the best.........the jeweller Mikko Milligan fashioned a silver aeroplane that he presented to me after the shoot." (Hellraiser)

→ 3   → 3A   → 4

GINGER BAKER'S

AIR FORCE

→ 12A

GINGER BAKERS
A.R. FORCE 2
33-3.43
PAYPOOER

Air Force

Influenced by the big band style prevalent in my youth, sometimes things got quite crazy! We once got involved in "…an enormous [bar room] brawl in which a bearded guy confronted me and I smashed my litre tankard across his face. Denny (Laine) was standing on the tables, jumping from one to the other, punching people as he went past……….the next thing I heard was Graham (Bond) telling everybody that he'd got a black belt in judo and that it had all 'got to stop'!" (GB & Hellraiser) (Hellraiser)

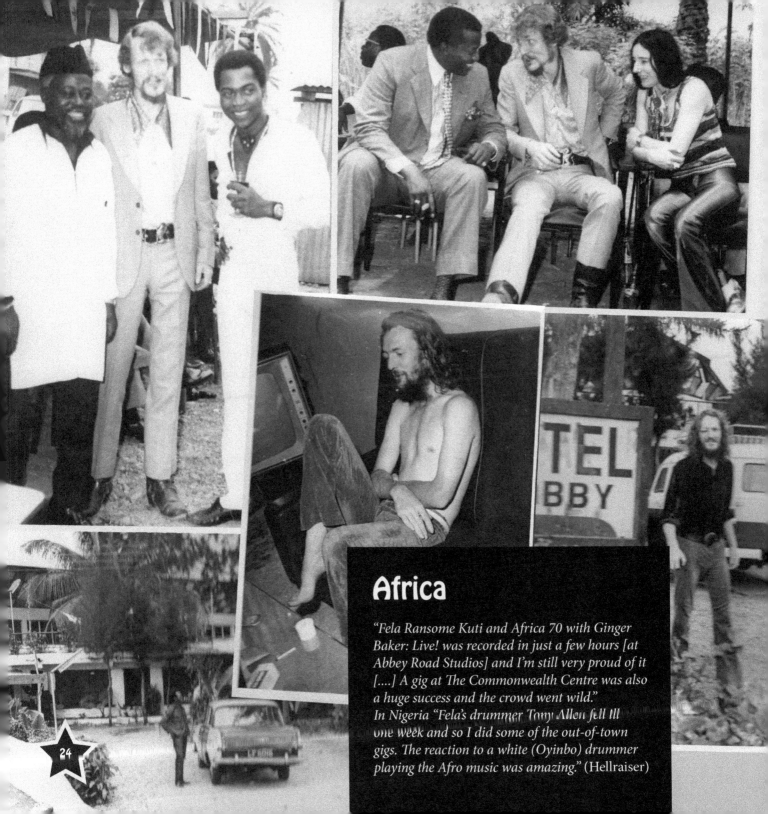

Africa

"Fela Ransome Kuti and Africa 70 with Ginger Baker: Live! was recorded in just a few hours [at Abbey Road Studios] and I'm still very proud of it [....] A gig at The Commonwealth Centre was also a huge success and the crowd went wild."
In Nigeria "Fela's drummer Tony Allen fell ill one week and so I did some of the out-of-town gigs. The reaction to a white (Oyinbo) drummer playing the Afro music was amazing." (Hellraiser)

Dem give am permit to carry baton

teargas

bullet

rifle

Dem fit carry basket for protection too

Na so we dey see am everyday

Na so he dey happen every time 2ce

One day One day

One Day one day

The whole thing charge

One day one day

Kalakuta show

Kalakuta show   2ce

Refrain . . . .

Dem make sure say dem

use their teargas, baton

and bullet (refrain)

Dem make sure say dem

use dem rifle, bullet

and teargas (refrain)

Dem make sure say dem

even carry dem basket

for protection too (Refrain)

Dem do one thing

Dem never do before 2ce

Dem hire axe o

Dem bring cutlas   2ce

Dem hire

awo o (2ce)

Borun wo o a wo lugbogbo

wa hen hen (2ce)

B'ole ya ko ya o

B'ole ya ko ya

B'ole do gun ka dogun o

B'ole do gun ko do gun

B'ole jose ko jose o

B'ole jose ko jose

Ojo p'ewe ikoko

Bo le ya ko ya

Ojo pe'we ikoko

Chorus Bo'le ya ko ya

B'ole dogun ko dogun o

Chorus B'ole ya ko ya

Bole j'ose ko j'ose o

Chorus: B'ole ya ko ya

DONT MAKE BIGMANISM

V — I — PISM TO ME

Boy, (Man), Donot cross my ways

as you like

Boy, (Man), Donot cross my ways

as you like . . . . . to please, amuse on

show off your powers importance

position . . . or what have you.

The proper owner of land (property), son of the soil,

always takes time . . . in stepping very gently

Gently, Gently Yeah — Yeah . . . . Gently, Gently

o o o o o o . . . . Gently (2ce)

Donot act, behave, please yourself with me,

AFRICA 70
PERSONNEL

Tony Allen
Leader Drumer

Lekan Animashaun
Baritone Sax

Tunde Williams
Trumphet

Henry Kofi
1st Konga

Christopher Uwaifor
Tenor Sax

Ogene Kologbo
Tenor Guitar

Ukem Stephen
2nd Trumphet

Franco Aboddy

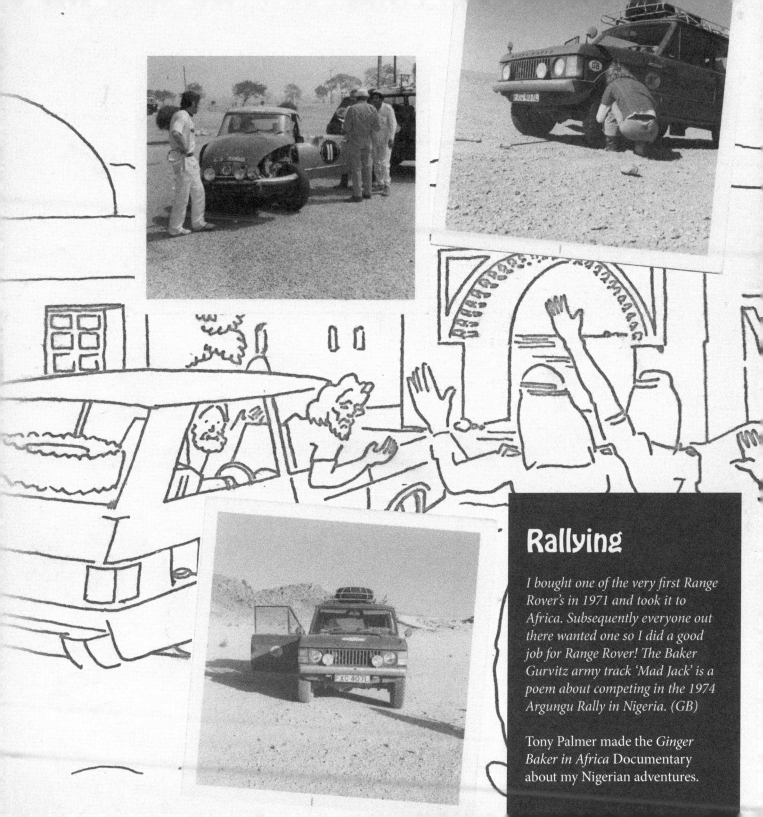

Rallying

I bought one of the very first Range Rover's in 1971 and took it to Africa. Subsequently everyone out there wanted one so I did a good job for Range Rover! The Baker Gurvitz army track 'Mad Jack' is a poem about competing in the 1974 Argungu Rally in Nigeria. (GB)

Tony Palmer made the *Ginger Baker in Africa* Documentary about my Nigerian adventures.

Wide wheels.   2.88 ratio
MKII Seats
MkII Leather wheel.

Headlight
Wiper blades
Hazard warning lights.
Rad leak at top.

P.E. Baker
01 - 422 2712

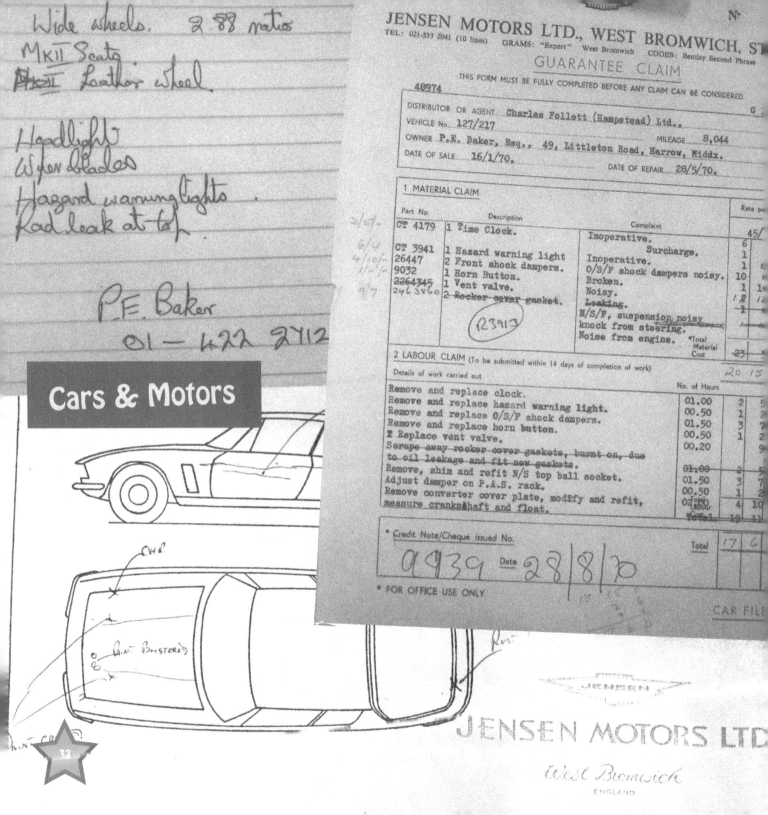

JENSEN MOTORS LTD., WEST BROMWICH, ST

TEL: 021-553 2041 (10 lines)   GRAMS: "Expert" West Bromwich   CODES: Bentley Second Phrase

GUARANTEE CLAIM

THIS FORM MUST BE FULLY COMPLETED BEFORE ANY CLAIM CAN BE CONSIDERED

48974

DISTRIBUTOR OR AGENT   Charles Follett (Hampstead) Ltd..
VEHICLE No. 127/217
OWNER P.E. Baker, Esq., 49, Littleton Road, Harrow, Middx.   MILEAGE   8,044
DATE OF SALE   16/1/70.   DATE OF REPAIR   28/5/70.

1 MATERIAL CLAIM

Part No.	Description	Complaint	Rate per
CT 4179	1 Time Clock.	Inoperative.	45/
CT 3941	1 Hazard warning light	Surcharge.	6
26447	2 Front shock dampers.	Inoperative.	1
9032	1 Horn Button.	O/S/F shock dampers noisy.	10
2264345	1 Vent valve.	Broken.	1
246 3860	2 Rocker cover gasket.	Noisy.	1/2
		Leaking.	1
	R3913	N/S/F, suspension noisy	
		knock from steering.	*Total Material
		Noise from engine.	Cost 23

2 LABOUR CLAIM (To be submitted within 14 days of completion of work)

Details of work carried out

	No. of Hours	
Remove and replace clock.	01.00	2
Remove and replace hazard warning light.	00.50	1
Remove and replace O/S/F shock dampers.	01.50	3
Remove and replace horn button.	00.50	1
Replace vent valve.	00.20	
Scrape away rocker cover gaskets, burnt on, due to oil leakage and fit new gaskets.	01.00	2
Remove, shim and refit N/S top ball socket.	01.50	3
Adjust damper on P.A.S. rack.	00.50	1
Remove converter cover plate, modify and refit, measure crankshaft and float.	02.00	4
	Labour Total 19	

* Credit Note/Cheque issued No.
9939   Date 28/8/70   Total   17   6

* FOR OFFICE USE ONLY

CAR FILE

JENSEN MOTORS LTD

West Bromwich
ENGLAND

DBM/SAC

JENSEN

REPAIR FILE COPY we were pleased to see you a
on Thursday, 27th August. Mr. R. A
D. B. Millard were hoping to be abl
as you know, they had to leave for

INVOICE TO

CONSIGNEE

P.E. Baker Esq,

		LH. " " Plinth.	CT3924
		Jensen Badge.	27644
			26254
	1 ea	Bonnet Top Moulding.	26793-2681
		LH. Sill Finisher.	26710

13 NOV 1970

The Robert Stigwood Organisation L...

Mr Millard,
Service Manager,
Jensen Motors Ltd.,
Spon Lane,
West Bromwich,
Birmingham.

119/099,

Dear Mr Millard,

     I am writing you you at the request of Mr Peter Baker - Ginger Baker, the drum star - about the hubs for his Jensen F.F. Mk. I.

     He says that some ten days ago you personally promised them to him "within 24 hours". As of writing this letter there is still no sign of them.

     I am sure I don't need to remind you that Mr Baker has been a long standing customer of Jensens, and indeed, your own publicity department has used pictures of him for promotional purposes.

     I would be glad if you could expedite these spares and perhaps let me know what is happening as Mr Baker has a very short fuse and may explode at any moment.

     Yours Faithfully,

     Robin Turner.

c.c. Richard Graves - Managing Director.

Please see my letter dated 13-11-70.
Copy for you for information. R.B.M

(Licensed annually by the City of Westminster)

34

DATE: 14/8/70 G/B   JOB NO. G198.

CAR RECOVERY SERVICE

Unit 10, Trumpers Way (Off Boston Rd.), Hanwell W.7

Tel: 574 6191/2 and 574 6882/3

Reg. No. YYH 27H

To transporting _Jensen_

from _Charles Follet_

to: _Jensen West Bro_

Charges Paid:

CONDITION OF CAR

Smashed.

CONTENTS OF CAR

☑ Spare Wheel ☑ Tools ☐ Jack ☐ Spot lights ☑ Wing Mirrors
☐ Radio ☑ Aerial ☐ Maps ☐ AA Book or RAC ☐ Leather
☐ Dusters ☐ Torch ☐ Keys ☐ Boot locked _Yes or No_

REG. NO. 127/217.
REG. NO. YYH. 27H.

PARTS REQUIRED FOR ABOVE REPAIR

ront Bumper Assy. Comp.	27724	84- 4- 0
ear " " "	73337	80- 0- 0
ot and Fog Lamps.	CT4637-CT4636	22- 8- 4
Side Flasher Lamp.	CT3924	4- 14- 2
" " " Plinth.	27644	2- 10- 6
nsen Badge.	26254	2- 13- 4
nnet Top Moulding.	26793-26811-26796	18- 17- 2
Sill Finisher.	26719	10- 10- 0
ctric Aerial and Lead.	CT6031-CT4433	

or letting me take

find this check OK!

ARROW, MX.
11/6/29

be different gear

was fitted either

ble to do this.

well I may get

view to having

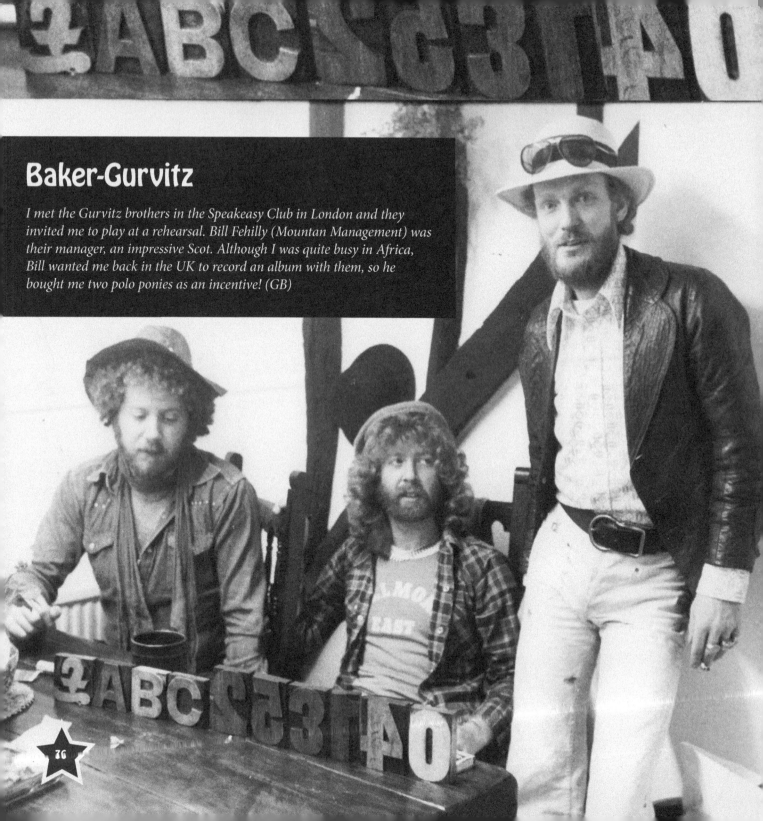

Baker-Gurvitz

I met the Gurvitz brothers in the Speakeasy Club in London and they
invited me to play at a rehearsal. Bill Fehilly (Mountain Management) was
their manager, an impressive Scot. Although I was quite busy in Africa,
Bill wanted me back in the UK to record an album with them, so he
bought me two polo ponies as an incentive! (GB)

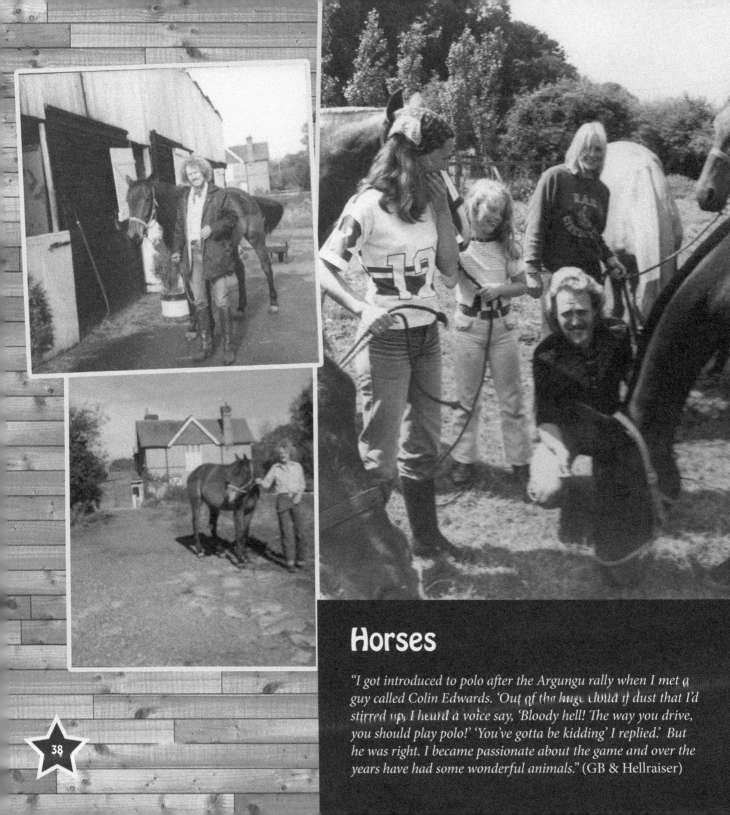

Horses

"I got introduced to polo after the Argungu rally when I met a guy called Colin Edwards. 'Out of the huge cloud of dust that I'd stirred up, I heard a voice say, 'Bloody hell! The way you drive, you should play polo!' 'You've gotta be kidding' I replied.' But he was right. I became passionate about the game and over the years have had some wonderful animals." (GB & Hellraiser)

Ginger man, horseman...

Ginger... with a favourite Polo pony

ON the green turf of Cowdray Park in Sussex hooves thud and the players wheel like jousting knights.

Polo, sport of kings and Princes of Wales, is in progress . . . including a most unlikely player. Distinguished —but not through any aristocratic blood.

He is Ginger Baker, red-haired, red-bearded and one of the world's best-known rock drummers.

Ginger's extraordinary talent on the drum-kit brought him early fame, crowned when he formed the legendary mid-'sixties group Cream with Eric Clapton and Jack Bruce.

When Cream eventually split up, he joined the short-lived Blind Faith, then created Ginger Baker's Air Force. Since then most of his work has been with African musicians.

His latest group is called The Dragonflies . . . who don't play any music at all. It is Ginger's own polo team, which reached tournament finals during Goodwood Week. Yet two years ago bricklayer's son Ginger had never even sat on a horse.

"If someone had told me then that I'd now be living and breathing polo, I would have laughed," said the wiry-framed Ginger, now 37. "But it's addictive — and I'm hooked."

Lord Cowdray—one of the wealthiest men in Britain— loaned Ginger his own ponies and secured his full-playing membership to the Cowdray Park Club.

COSTLY

Several of Ginger's mostly Argentinian-bred ponies are worth at least 3,000 guineas, and he estimates his stable to be worth around £20,000. The cost of keeping a team of polo ponies runs into thousands per season.

"It's quite a financial struggle for me to stay in the game," he admitted.

At the end of the British season, Ginger is planning to visit the Argentine, the Mecca of world polo. Like most rock super-stars he's been advised to leave Britain and its punitive taxes.

"I don't want to leave," he says. "But I might have to stay there until I can afford to live in England again."

Whether he'll eventually settle for drum sticks or polo sticks is something Ginger will have to beat time over.

cream

It was always, simply, Cream. No need for a definite article. There were the Beatles and the Rolling Stones but it was never the Cream.

Like all the best names, this one functioned at more than one level. It suggested superlative qualities, an elite grouping of the choicest elements. In America, it implied the defeat of all competition. At a deeper and less conscious level, it invoked the pleasure principle, indulgent, richly satisfying, dionysian.

... described were, for their audi-
... dividual instruments, the
... ip.

... e early summer of 1966.
... circuit was that Eric
... 45), so recently raised to
... erie of fans, would leave
... to form a group with Jack
... er (born August 19, 1939)
... with the Graham Bond
... orn May 14, 1943), who'd
... Bluesbreakers, was current-
... ed Mann.

... igh regard of their fellow musicians. But Clapton's preeminence as the country's supreme blues guitarist created the keenest public antici- pation and high expectations of the imminent trinity. Such a combination of talent, and its promise of future excel- lence, caused their followers to talk of a "group's group."

Ironically, in March 1966 the pop journal *Melody Maker* had conducted a poll among Britain's top groups to nominate their ideal six-piece band. Eric Clapton and Ginger Baker were the choices for lead guitar and drums, but Jack Bruce was beaten by the Who's bass guitarist, John Entwistle.

With the idea adrift in the ether, it's perhaps no sur- prise that a couple of months later, Ginger approached Eric about forming just such an elite band. Driven by similar thoughts of evolving from straight blues into a new kind of pop music, the guitarist's sole proviso

was that Jack Bruce must be the band's bassist.

Speculation was rife as to the music that three such volatile personalities would create. Both Ginger Baker and Jack Bruce had long musical pedigrees, with leanings toward jazz; Baker revered America's Buddy Rich and Elvin Jones and was inspired by England's Phil Seamen, while Bruce had wielded double bass in a Scottish jazz band before joining Baker for a time in Alexis Korner's Blues Incorporated. Eric Clapton's mentors came exclusive- ly from the blues world, but he instinctively sought the freedom of his new partners' more open discipline.

When interviewed, Clapton was adamant: "What we want to do is anything that people haven't done before. Most people have formed the impression of us as three solo musicians clashing with each other. We want to can- cel that idea and be a group that plays together."

The band, dubbed Cream by Clapton at its initial rehearsal, made its first major public appearance at the Sixth National Jazz and Blues Festival at Windsor on July 3, 1966. An ecstatic audience overlooked the trio's lack of preparation. "We were just scrambling for the forefront," said Clapton, "and we didn't get much feedback until we played in front of an audience. That was when we real- ized that they actually wanted to go off somewhere. And we had the power to take them."

Cream's first single, "Wrapping Paper," as subtly dispos- able as its title, deliberately undercut its fans' expectations. More to their taste, the album *Fresh Cream*, released in December 1966, combined blues standards such as "I'm So Glad, "From Four Until Late" and "Spoonful" with new compositions, "N.S.U.," "Sleepy Time Time" and "Sweet Wine." Vehicles for Clapton's intense blues guitar tech- nique were contrasted with more formally structured melodies from the team of Jack Bruce and Pete Brown.

Both strands met in the group's second single, "I Feel Free," as ethereal harmonies and sustained guitar notes floated over a driving rhythm. It was an original and excit- ing sound that took them into Britain's Top 20.

Although the band needed the lifeblood of popular

Hall of Fame 1993

"The rehearsals were pretty good and very enjoyable. But we had to sit for hours at a table while all these other idiots like Jim Morrison's band picked up their awards. They made long speeches saying 'I'd like to thank my mother and my uncle who lent me 50 bucks 20 years ago, my kids, my animals and my dog's granddad…' Each had this whole list of people they wanted to thank! Every one was doing this and they were all a load of wankers. Despite this, I quite enjoyed sitting with Naomi Campbell, who was with Eric at the time. I really liked her. When it finally came to our turn, my back was aching from sitting on an uncomfortable chair for ages listening to these silly speech makers so I just said 'well everybody's said it all, so…."thanks, guys" and that was it. The actual gig wasn't as good as it could've been but it was ok." (Hellraiser)

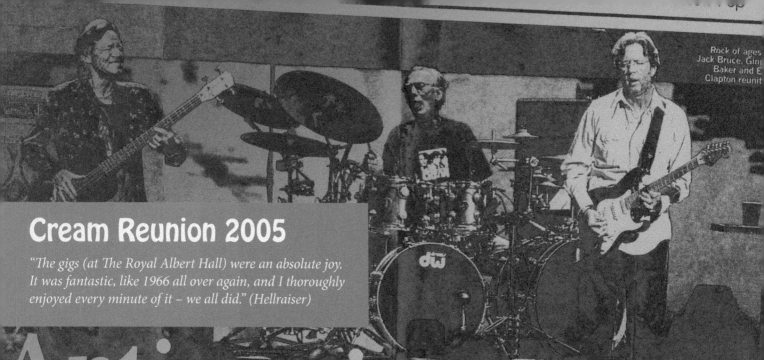

Rock of ages
Jack Bruce, Gin[...]
Baker and E[...]
Clapton reunit[...]

Cream Reunion 2005

*"The gigs (at The Royal Albert Hall) were an absolute joy.
It was fantastic, like 1966 all over again, and I thoroughly
enjoyed every minute of it – we all did." (Hellraiser)*

Anti-ageing Cream

*'With Carlos Santana,
Nettie & my nephew Ken
back stage MSG 2005.
Carlos is a good friend.'*

Door
Loggia

Seat

No Support / This Event is Being Filmed
Fri, 06 May 2005
At 8:00 PM

Promoter
£175.00

CREAM

ROYAL ALBERT HALL, LONDON
Mon. 2nd, Tues. 3rd, Thur. 5th and Fri. 6th May 2005
ON SALE: MONDAY 31st JANUARY 9am

Zildjian Awards (2008)

"Charlie Watts has always been a real musician in my opinion and a wonderful guy as well" (Hellraiser)

AAA

mf

mean fiddler

artist
GINGER BAKER

date
04/11/09

venue
JAZZ CAFE

Jazz Café (2009)

Stevie and I played together for the first time in decades at a party for my 70th Birthday, he's a real 'jazzer'! (GB)

Eric came to visit me at my birthday gig; here we are back stage with his former girlfriend, model & artist Charlotte Martin. (GB)

...and a peaceful new year
Love from
Paul and Linda McCartney
and Wings

Family Pics

"I first met Linda in the USA in 1968. Wings recorded part of 'band on the run' at my Lagos studio; but EMI quickly put a stop to this..." (GB)

LINDA'S PICTURES

Hello Ginger + family —
Remember the '61 days?
Here's your BOOK

Love

Linda
London '76

"Our first family holiday as rich folks (and indeed first family holiday at all), had been to Mexico City and Acapulco in 1967, where Dad had delighted in cutting crabs in half with a large machete, until my mother stopped him."

Nettie Baker (memoir)

Nettie in Neasden (in the room where Cream was born), with some of my sculptures on the shelf above' (GB)

'Steve Marriott's widow Toni at Nettie's wedding, My son Kofi worked with Steve extensively as his drummer in the late 1980's & was very upset by his death.'

Nettie's Wedding (1991)

54

Me with mum... (1990)

With Granddaughter Zara (1994)

My sister Pat,
3rd right, with
Nettie & nieces
Cheryl & Jaqui
(2014)

My wife Kudzai

Zara & I in NYC 2005

Last pic of family together (Denver, USA 1997)

Dinner with
Nettie & Leda

View from the Bandwagon at dawn...(1961)

P.Baker

Paintings & drawings

Totem Pole Carving

"...I had a studio in the loft of my new house where I did my wood carving." (Hellraiser)

For some reason my first wife Liz later painted this particular carving green & used it as a garden ornament! But originally I fashioned it from a single piece of wood. On one occasion, the chisel slipped and went through my finger severing the nerves and tendon. I woke the whole house by running down the ladder from the loft, shouting 'get a tourniquet!' at 2 o' clock in the morning'! (GB)

Dobi
for Moi

P.Baker '64

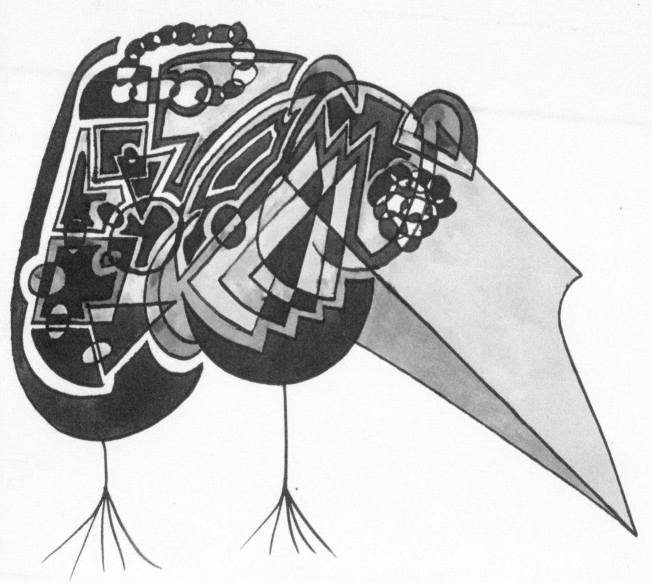

(25)
24.4.1968

Recently discovered paintings from the 60's...

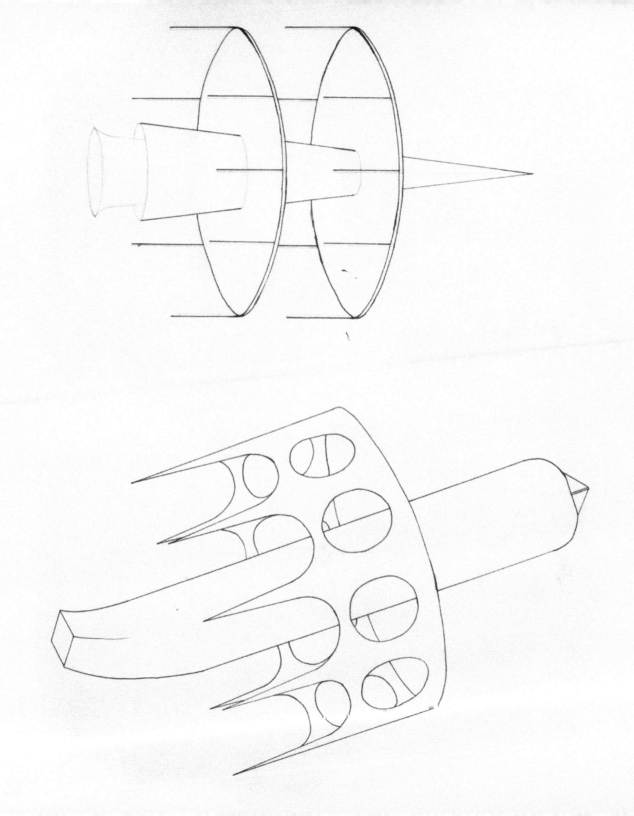

"In memory of my first wife Liz who passed away in March 2014"
Ginger Baker

Special Thanks to all the record companies who so kindly participated in this project.
'A Drummer's Tale' conceived by Ginger Baker and Steve Tannett with Curation and invaluable assistance from Nettie Baker.
Original paintings & drawings by Ginger Baker. Front cover art by Liz Baker.
Graphic Design: Dylan Martin at friedbanana.co.uk
Artwork Photography: Marcos Bevilacqua Photo slides: Gavin Bambrick at Photofusion

Ginger Baker would like to thank the following people for their help in making this project possible:

Julian Huntly and the team at Pledge Music, Stewart Copeland, Alec Dankworth, Pee Wee Ellis, Abass Dodoo,
Cecil Offley, Leda Baker, Jeff Chegwin, Sid Truelove, Charlotte Martin, Andrew Leighton Pope, Nick Berry, Penny Ganz,
Andy and the team at Live Nation, DW Drums, Zildjian, Classic Rock Magazine, Paul Farberman (USA) & All the photographers.

Espresso Songs Ltd, 56 Compton Street, London EC1V0ET   WWW.ESPRESSOSONGS.COM   WWW.GINGERBAKER.COM

Lightning Source UK Ltd.
Milton Keynes UK
UKHW050243121019
351361/UK00005B/24/P